I0160030

Snake Eyes

by 1st 5th Remote Viewer

Phantom Ops - Psi trained by Military

www.nuts4mars.com

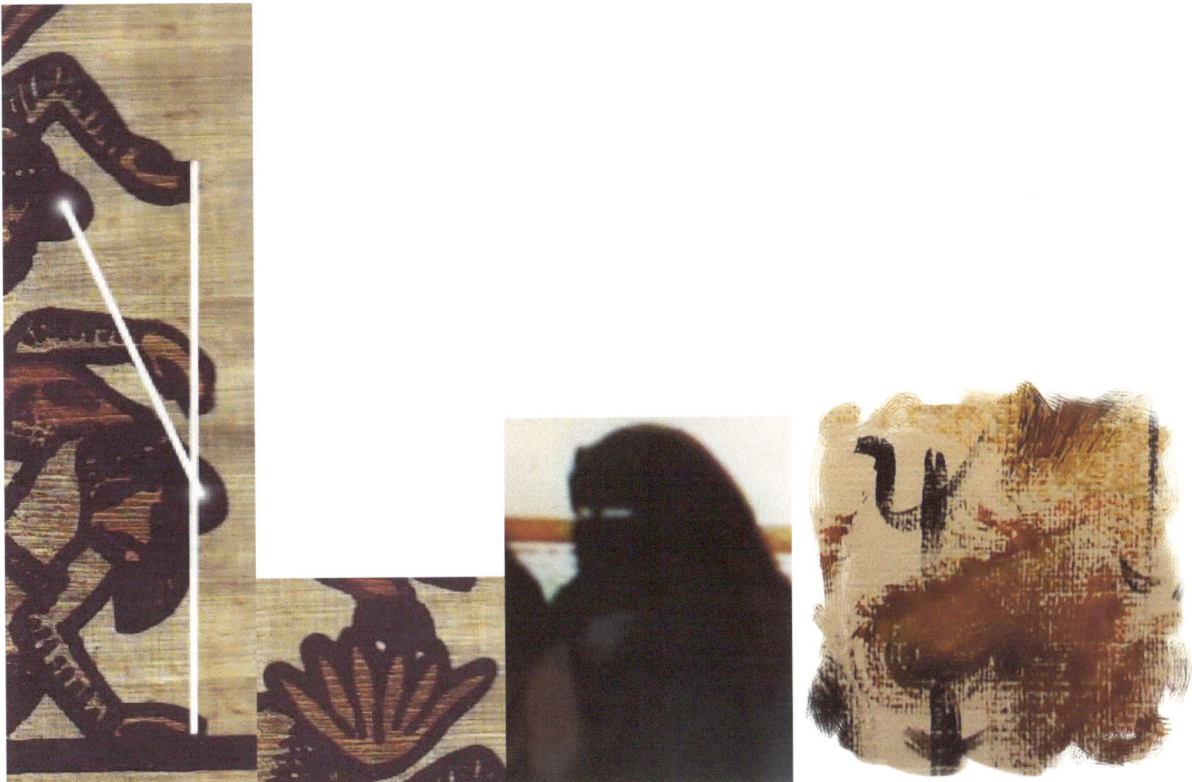

ISBN# 978-0-9813261-5-3   Copyright © 1st 5th 2010

INTRODUCTION

As a Remote Viewer, I (aka -1st 5th) first started to decipher the mystery of the Quantum 5th Dimensional ability to view an object and/or it's associated event content, in the early 1980s. With only a few University courses in Philosophical studies, Classical Mythology and Psychology, and having already a substantial background as a creative artist, a painter. As an artist a full time sober painter a creative artist not a copy artist a purely creative talent, I was painting full time and realizing that there was a whole 'otherness' a new thing happening and then set out to develop the backwards look at figuring out what it was. With Psychic Precognition skills, visual imagery, intensive full internal visuals, and what Immanuel Kant the German Philosopher called 'intuitive-logic'.

For example in the book 'Star Script' by 1st 5th, it explains how early on I perceived and understood the use of 'gap' and 'direction', 'reversals' and Absolute principles. They come into play with the necker shift, it is *holistic*. I got that, took a while it wasn't a mainstream work at the time, nor was necker shift, these were done when it was still the 4th see Dr. Rudolph v.b. Ruckers book 'Geometry, Relativity and the 4th Dimension' …it was predating our modern Personal Computers by about 10 years there was no digital world as we have it now, and the www was not invented yet.

To understand what the actual Quantum Psychic or what I call Q5 Leap is about, you are best to read the books on it, accessed from my website, www.nuts.4mars.com . Skim the fluff. Go for the 'gosh look, that's what it is doing' discovery parts. I am unfolding and developing the basic understanding to the Physical Quantum structure of the Hypershift phenomenon. An all pervasive and precision Space Light and Time Light combined or separated inherent in different View encapsulations.   There are other Mathematicians and Physical Theorists would do the actual figuring in far greater depth. This work covers raw basics only, as they are seen and understood. Sometimes it takes years for some part of the process that has been revealing to present with the Eureka moment.

Additionally there was extremely intensive computer pixel visual recognition and release whereby you had to link the Psi painting color, shape and cohesive parts to the photos that were provided as containing the matching material in the particular time frame, to each Remote Viewing session. This work involved two plus years of extensive training by the Military. It is an arduous process requiring concentration, commitment, immersion, isolation, and psychic parameters. Not to be undertaken by the hobbyist or fan. The Star Trail that unfolded by undertaking this adventure was a life long pursuit, as a creative artist with a strong focus painting and reading a ton of science fiction, as well as later on taking University courses in Astronomy, Physics and Mathematics to aid in the development of the understanding and skills necessary. All in all a fascinating and rewarding occupation, assisting with the security components inherent in each View piece.

There is script involved as well, not just painting; Q5 Leap audio/visual. RV is a learned and trained highly encoded process requiring familiarity and Shadow Ops procedures to decode and appreciate timely relevance as it pertains to matters of 'seeing' tips and clues, much like a regular Psychic Detective. Although, myself I vastly prefer to focus on the Deepside of Inter-Galactic realms reading the Star Trail. The Military and other Earthly security and protection forces are inseparable from this fascinating Oracle unfolding.

This particular account, *Snake Eyes,* begins with some interesting divulgences from the Spyland ops that is usually kept behind the scenes. Given it's timely relevance I have decided in this work to allow some small glimpse into the workings of the Oracle for the most part it's typed streaming (language - audio) Remote Viewing, along with one Psi Paint, 8"x10" oil on canvas/pad, done using the trained by Military process, and then decoded as it relates to the issues of security we encounter constantly. Good old Earth being such as it is there is no shortage of work, whether bad guys, unfortunate events or just plain odd happenings.

Canadian Soldier Afghanistan; matching Psi Painting descriptive visual marker 'emote'

Shadow Ops - Notes & visuals on the Cordoba Mosque NY, NY revealing Links between Imam Feisal Rauf and Radical Islamic Terrorism - by 1ˢᵗ 5ᵗʰ

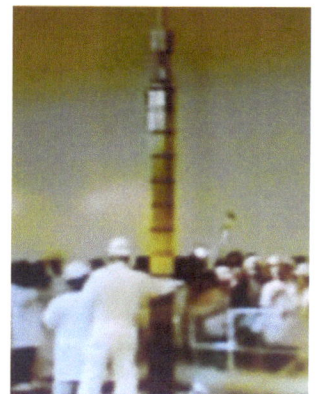

Cordoba Islamic Mosque location, not dice form top right; another ancient link; Iran nukes dice

Here, check this out, the new proposed mosque that Islam wants in New York would go right here at this building with the 'snake eyes' dice visual dots showing on the side. Me, I think it is a sign that they are a Terror Cult and that old papyrus the Chariot just nailed them for it. The book 'Coming Forth By Day' also wrongly translated as 'Book of the Dead' actually mentions it as does the Bible, talking about a Terror Cult operating in ancient times. Well in modern times, that is just what Bin Laden who it is said also has a liking for ancient Egyptian things, was into. As well as many of their top leaders hailing from Egypt. Reviving the Terror part of their old formed religious/political tradition. Passing it off on their illiterate as a 'holy war' and the silly Fatwas reinforcing that slant, perpetrating an abominable way of looking at life, no more than a Death Cult. Snake eyes, and a roll of the dice …not going to replace our freedom loving living cultures.

Psi is tea leaf readable if you have any psi you can develop it and then do just about anything maybe not marble tossing but anything with a pattern or swirls like in scrying or smoky crystals. You don't actually use a clear one crystal you go for something with patterns. Sure fire smoke would do but it moves a bit fast you wouldn't get much you want something that has some weight to it. Tea leaves settled to a bottom after it's drained of liquid. Not squinting through the water watching moving tea leaves. You have to have a focus for your psi to get images and patterns to read. I sometimes see 'more than is there' it's psychic viewing not just looking at the page. Funny as that sounds, it's a concentration point focus for your inner eye along with your natural, developed, psychic ability. Linking to the images the glimpses of what's ahead. But they need the psi to actually do the Viewing not just decoding. You can't just drink tea and read colourful meaning into the leaves' patterns. We are not manifesting spooky.
You can get a psychic to read patterns and views from focusing on them, or you can do what we do here use the psychic to paint the psi sensed and encoded emotives with RV elements that we learn and work with . For a happy decoder.
Painted by a Viewer so there is sense there that is psi linked to read. You won't just go to a Library start opening books with a reader and making any real links as psi unless that reader was psi and maybe just not a painter. That's possible too. Edgar Cayce lay down and talked. Someone else took notes. Clairvoyance was when he just read from the air nothing there. He also did books but he misunderstood and thought he did some kind of osmosis by sleeping on them. That's not it. I use books for RV too. It's prophecy that links together and surfaces. I just open them. Most often I get a hit. It's just how it is. It's not just books.
Q5 Psi surfaces. But the Quantum goes through substance spacetimelight it zips along and fetches. Then you are drawn to it. You sense it then fetch it is more how to put it. That's what I happening. It's new in the depth of our understanding the computers make it a timely surfacing of our knowledge that papyrus without the computer would be just an interesting composition I might read some angles and surface features but not the hot RV encapsulation that I am getting in fact from it It's Computer time linked in order for us to understand it. No computers no Q5 Leap. It was simplified prophecy Oracle and then the Remote Viewing of the early Former CIA project Stargate phenomenon. This is a more sophisticated Q5 leap development due to the modern era of digital computers.

'Rambo' starring Sylvester Stallone, snakes at the start, RV paints

Ancient Egyptian hieroglyph 'teleport' visuals?

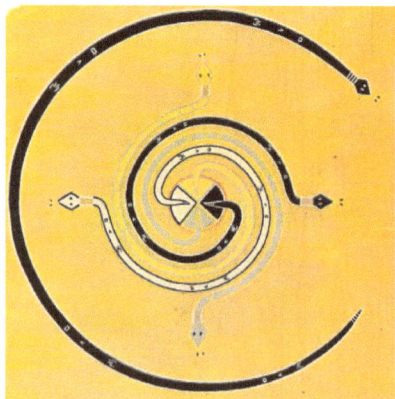

Navajo sand painting Psi; Photo of door/bricks showing an overt snake head pattern; snake head

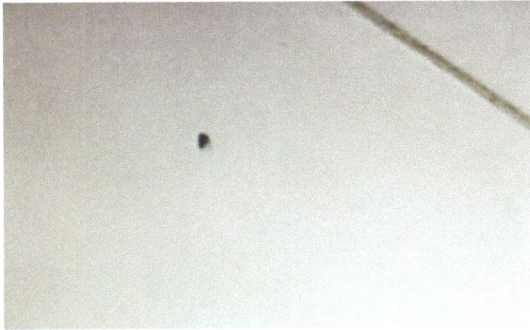

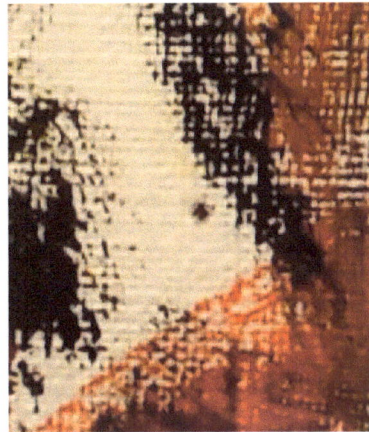

Aug 24 bullet hole El Paso Texas 30 yards from Juarez, Mexico

SB1070 PROTESTERS BLOCKADE
SHERIFF ARPAIO'S JAIL

Down Mexico Way – Violence over the Border into the South Western States
Arizona Sheriffs – Sheriff Joe Arpaio Maricopa County; (below) Larry Dever, Cochise County

Ground Zero Islamic (Cordoba) Mosque Imam Feisal;
Arizona Sheriffs Larry Dever, Cochise County & Paul Babeu, Pinal County AZ,

Arranged visual chat symbols beside the Imam; they are like Eskimos cleaning a whale,
the desert cultures using it all, systematically; note the match to the sheriff's badge

Corner square measure; Note- Faisal the Times Square May 1st, 2010 attempted bomber,
solid links to Radical Islam Terrorists also displayed visuals using T Squares that
architects use.
The symbol at the right is a reversed Mars symbol used in Astrology & Astronomy still;
Current angst over the 'Mars claim' by the Viewer 1st 5th see 'Knights of Mars' for details

The use of the squared spiral, snake coils, and squarish snake head visual images.

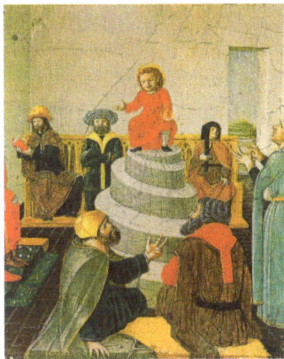

RV surfaced material –note the corner square and squared cloth; match on the headpiece of the man at right on the page and enlarged above; Imam Feisal Rauf on trip note corner square cloth

Ancient Egyptian head dress Uraeus Snake on front; snake heads from *Chariot papyrus*

Ground Zero Mosque Imam Feisal; corner round 'square' pattern, squared 'eyes' snake chat visual;

May 1ˢᵗ Times Square New York, NY- attempted bomber Faisal Shazad links to Radical Islamic Jihad; in the background behind him, (photo left) is the same pattern they are apparently using as chat, a visual descriptive for *corner round*. It's like the cops do, they often go *around the corner*.

Radical Islamic Taliban Terrorist super bad guy Hakeemullah

-supposedly killed in Jan 2010, he resurfaced on May 1st same day as the Time Square bomber.

There was an Islamic Caliphate meeting at the Chicago Hilton with similar snake visuals
in 2009. This terrorist's name is Hakeemullah, they had 'URL' on a banner outside the meeting.

RV called #9; Faisal Shazad photo ops #9 behind, Bulleyes in front; showing access to RV info

A Sample of ancient Egyptian snake hieroglyphs -

Q5 leap of snake glyph emote

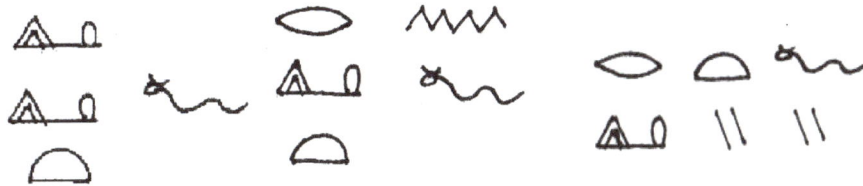

'one who may/will hear'

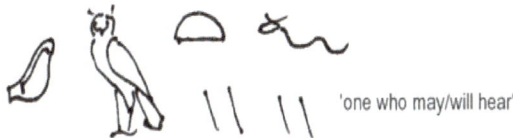

'one who may/will see'

*

'ddt' what he gives (present); 'rdit.n' what he gave (past); 'rdity.f' one who may/will give (future)

*one who may/will hear, one who may/will see; they had one for 'read'

(masc.)
p f : that

(fem)
tf : that

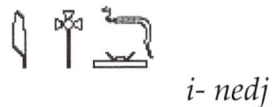

i- nedj

-the feather (i) = truth; the symbol next to it 'ned' is an unknown

Major General John F. Campbell, Commander Screaming Eagles, 101st Airborne;
(above, right) enlarged from Afghan. Flag, note the corner square/round visuals

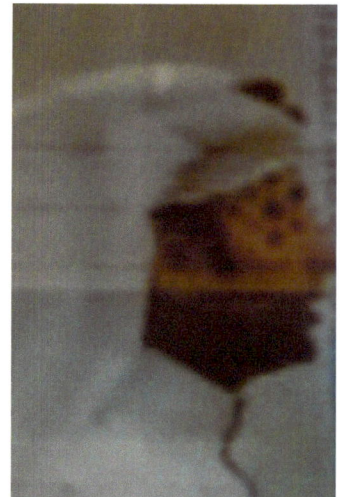

Q5 Leap psi paint of black suicide vest displayed by Maj Gen Campbell; hair visual
match; Note - 'eagle' arrangement of head gear on man standing beside Imam Feisal;
given their using the 'corner square/round' visual for chat with terrorists, appears it also
links to the conflict in Afghan.

Ground Zero Cordoba Mosque New York NY, Imam Feisal Rauf- behind him, 'triangle visual with bottom left and right corners chopped, slanted. Visual match to tower airport and the round top of the same involved air port tower, was already showing, with Rauf on his trip chat signal with Saudis the other day,

Feisal Rauf looking like 'in an airport lobby' luggage **behind,** note - they started using backgrounds for chat

To finish off, we noted the top of the tree with the V for his 'victory' chat, Fmr Gov. Sarah Palin bigger V

Islam is largely illiterate. So, the guys who can't read would do those visual lines as 'snakes' ..so they must have wanted them to feel involved (just makes sense) belonging to their common cause so they got using the lettering as Snakes. The Dots as Eyes. So they didn't sound condescending. Not wanting to alienate tribal leaders in particular. Likely seen as a necessary adjustment, not just a nicety.

James Mosque 5 – Iran Esfahan; 'peach pit' visual pattern match, enlarged

Note the grey line for shadow ops and slant -the candy stripe on the kid, balloon, his microphone; Feisal Rauf chatting with Shadow far left bottom corner....

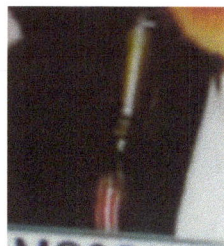
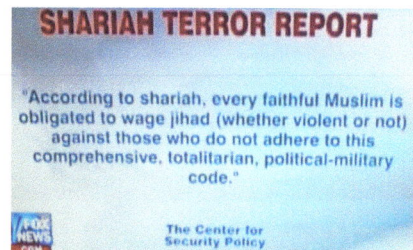

SHARIAH TERROR REPORT

"According to shariah, every faithful Muslim is obligated to wage jihad (whether violent or not) against those who do not adhere to this comprehensive, totalitarian, political-military code."

The Center for Security Policy

OF GZ MOSQUE
SLUMLORD BY NJ CITY
AN UPSET VIC

Shadow 'chat'

Note how they removed the usual Religious inclusion, wording and reworked it as political/Military. The Enemy itself with their version and it is their Holy War, would have used the words political-religious. I feel until they start being honest and stop the political lie fest here on N. American soil they won't have a hope of ever fixing it seriously to make as in force the bad guys of radical o Islamic intolerance and mandated objections to other than Islamic faith and behaviour, to allow for the rest of the planet. There are others here, these guys don't get a pass on that one. It's inevitable, they have to face the facts and get it right. No, they can't just object to the rest of us being different. That's just common sense necessity or they get to live under a nice big old dome. Or maybe, Venus…here on Earth, Islam is going to have to look in the mirror and get a serious grip. Removing words to make it sound more friendly than it is hardly does it. Try a nice healthy dose of Reality 101. They have to modernize. Not exactly unheard of, Christian religious faith did some serious Reforms throughout history. We weren't just at our current stage right off. Things advanced on Earth as we went along. These fighters and troublemakers and anti modern world need to address their own blame for error and decide to deal honestly.

If they don't modernize and decide to stay to Old Islam without the rest of the world they can't tell us what to do. They will have to just implode in their own lands, out of gross over population and impoverishment. Not up to us we can only do the best we can for them. The rest is up to them . If they decide to just stay old Stone Age savages then so be it. But if that is the direction they go in, we will need to rethink any assistance aimed at modernizing people who refuse to take out that totally horrific Jihad mandate to convert and /or kill any non Muslims! We would want them isolated and not in contact with our people so they didn't spread that into our lands and their hatred of our culture causing trouble for us. They can do as they please ultimately but they can't walk all over us. We need leaders who are concerned first and foremost with our people in our lands retaining our freedom and culture of creativity and tolerance. They do NOT get to merge in their blind intolerance. It's totally unacceptable for us over here or any other lands of advanced civilization, to just put blindfolds on and sing while they plan their slaughter. They don't want to change and accept others? Fine. Then keep them OUT and away from the rest of us.

Ontario, Canada and France, and Belgium have *banned* the burkas coverings and enforcements. Ontario banned Sharia itself. Recently in Oklahoma, USA the citizens voted on a referendum that passed by 70%, to ban Sharia permanently. However, their right to their vote's outcome was usurped by Muslims who are focused on only allowing for Sharia Law not Western Law and are now taking them to Court over it.

Location of proposed Victory Mosque NY, NY. Tail end of the street match to Chariot papyrus excerpt with the obvious visual ...Of a tilted building that has a pattern like the one at far left end of street and the escalate theme.

Corner Round - RV training visual code

The Military trained me and access the Oracle, daily. Nasa is anti war, it's an ongoing thing. They link into the Media via CNN and people like Amanpour. The same one who was horrified and emotionally upset a few years ago that Israel was sitting having tea with Lebanese Army and not 'fighting' like Hezbollah! Clear cut case of 'whose side are you on'. it wasn't ours.

As for the abuse of the Spyland tools, that's happened before. There was a JAG case in Court over their RNM Remote Neural Monitoring before. details at -
www.iahf.com/nsa/20010214.html

UPDATE: *January 17th, 2011 Imam Rauf has been replaced as Cordoba Project head, 'due to a Speaking Tour interfering with his working on it full time'.*

'Snake Eyes' starring Nicholas Cage and Gary Sinise

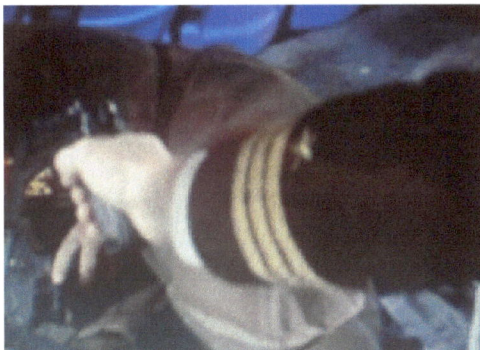

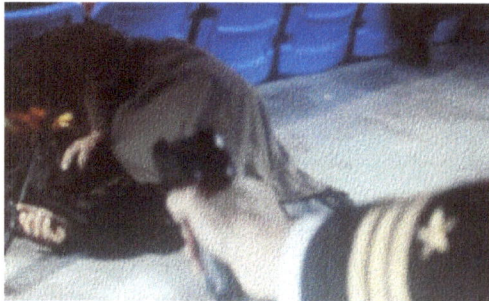

RV of arm with stripes on it match to scene with Gary Sinise

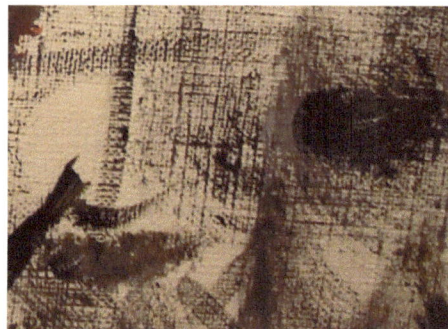

Large ball from end scene 'Snake Eyes'

Gary Sinise – matching structure to the RV cage; cell phone electromagnetic shield cage (below, right)

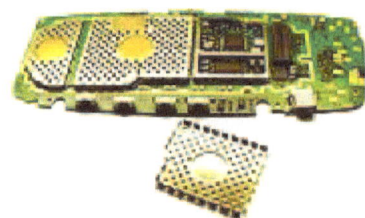

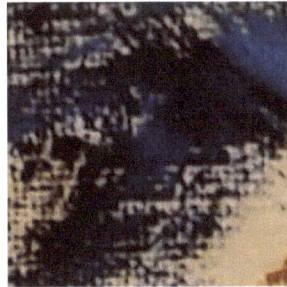

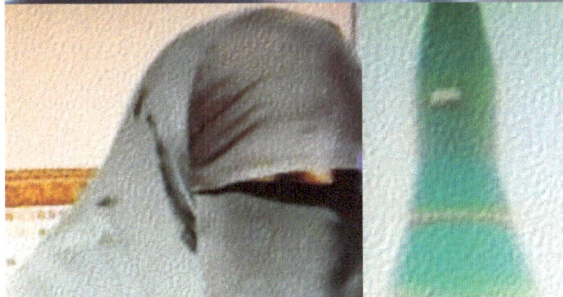

Enemy Jihadist current conflict eye slits and a Nuke slot; Q5 Leap time synch RV

The following pages deal with some of the rampant misapplication of secret ops tools. A true nightmare scenario of subliminal influence methods, and former stealth communication devices being abused and secretly being weaponized. The reality of the Oracle vision of a certain path of horrific consequence, realized.

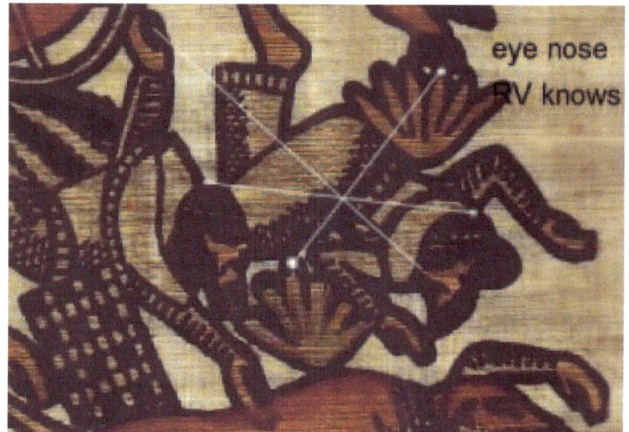

Matrix Reloaded & Matrix Revolutions (top) ~ starring Keanu Reeves; Chariot excerpt
Full Chariot ancient Egyptian hieroglyphic papyrus in 'TIME LEAP' by 1st 5th

Iraq Aug 22/2010 Bullets being loaded; Matrix Reloaded RV

Bullets

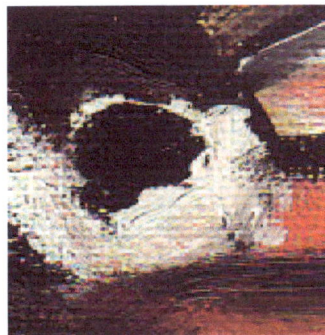

2006 Christian artefact RV; Jesus Ossuary (Israel Antiquities Authority) recently discovered

Sky Trails by CF-18 Hornets over Q5 leap photo by 1st 5th

Glass using Tiffany method, copper foil and lead soldering. Filled with water and hung in the direct sunlight it makes prism rainbow splotches of color. This one has water sedimentation marks, usually it's clear glass. You can see the obvious pattern match. That's how RV passes along tips. Patterns and descriptives and emotes the small stick figures who are showing emotions and 'doing' things. We decode as in Read the sensed cohesion of the visual messaging, to try to make sense of what the visuals are saying. Like trying to decipher Nostradamus' quatrains. Additionally you can see the Precision Marker RV of the hand 'inserted' into the form. Read as it appears visually, as 'insertions', ie: subliminal input to subconscious.

A submarine- note row of single file people on it, and in the Chariot excerpt (above, left and right)

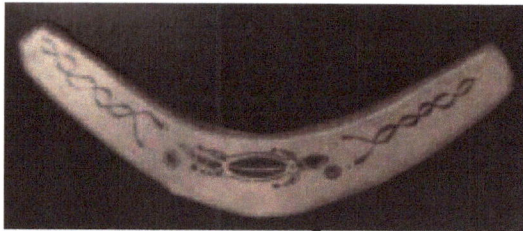

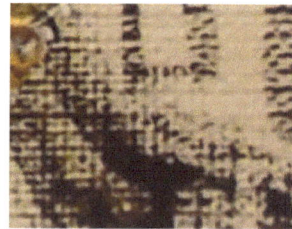

Australian boomerang RV & psi paint matching front curve

Authentic (Raiders of the Lost Ark starring Harrison Ford, style) Australian kangaroo Bullwhip Handcrafted by Si Davey http://sidaveywhips.com; Chariot papyrus excerpt

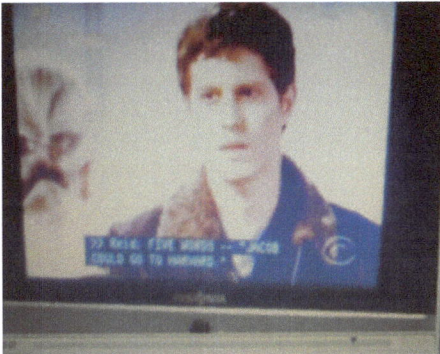

USA Senator Harry Reid (Nevada) eye - boy and hidden script; subliminal hidden insert
during day time Soap on Global Edmonton television, I kid you not, and if you hit pause you
Could see the words read - >> *REID: FIVE WORDS - - 'JACOB COULD GO TO   HARVARD' "*

Theatre with the 'evil eye' in stone pattern on it that they seem so fascinated with, note BABA in script

Info on that old CIA former Stargate with the experiments mentioned on Sonar and
Remote Neural Monitoring and even a bit on insertions, can be found online; some at
www.remoteviewed.com/crv_manual.htm read through it, not at all what the training
is like now, this developed exponentially with computers. But it gives you an idea into
it and the direction they were going and shows the words and lines that they did in
fact develop remote viewing, now understood as Quantum 5th D Psi.

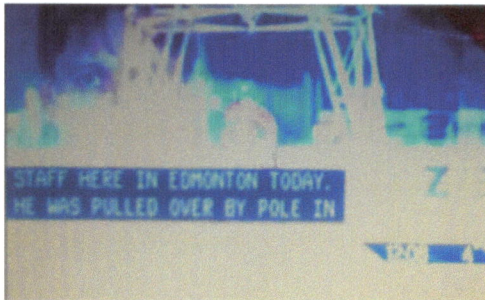

Hidden subliminal script on noon Global News; Bridge art piece in gallery beside Theatre/eye

Note the small boy and Eye showing upper left corner and the bridge in the center of the screen. It was the noon news on Global; it's a hidden subliminal insertions meant to operate like the low audio they have on those new ager non smoking tapes …you hear the music they run the subliminals under them for the subconscious mind to pick up on and be influenced. They ran them in the 1060s at the theatres during intermission as salty popcorn to get the audience to go buy soft drinks. They were banned completely decades ago. Seems these guys are in reinventing subliminal land. They blew up a bridge and murdered people over in Iraq that same day, using a suicide bomber. (above, right) A painting of a bridge, in the window of the commercial gallery next to the Theatre with BABA on it. Front and center, only one there, same timing.

Minnay Lodge campsite, Yemen - Remote View by 1st 5th Psi painting Dec 2009

Kandagal Village, Afghanistan, RV color/structure form (at left of center, in photo)

VIEW: '#9' from 1985; darkened line to highlight the one running alongside it in the View, enlarged; air strike on Zarqawi June 7th, 2006 Northeast of Baghdad; they dropped 2 500 lb bombs on al Zarqawi. You can see the 'rounded corner' in the photo (below, left) probably why they are so hot on chatting using that for their new pattern favourite, the 'rounded corner', marks their Revenge specifically.

As for the Muslims in on the Jihad fights, check out the chat going on with cloth and 'orbs with dots (reflections of light) in snake eyes positions. The 'paid to be politically correct experts' are calling it an orb and the sign that the Yemeni Jihad was 'going global'.

USA - WH

Now isn't that cute? And their American 'experts' and I use the term loosely, said in reply to it being pointed out, that the attack on the Saudi Prince using PETN like the packages coming out of Yemen just recently, *was a sign that they went global.* It sure is. Whatever they're on, give me some! Next is a photo of Awlaki clicking his fingers like on a camera, and then the photo they put up over the Yemen packages also of PETN, with golly gee, look Ethel another of them round dark orbs patterns with the wow reflections like, super FX and more snake eyes!

(Below) Awlaki clicking an 'air camera' video and his dark glasses/reflection dots Orb.

Saudi Arabian King Abdullah and entourage; snake eyes pattern; sword with orb/eyes emote

Look, more of the 'we like eyes' from the bad guy, the one who replaced the Mehsuds the drones took out, over in Khyber Pass, Pakistan's Taliban area. Only in this one under the cloth obvious goat eye folding arrangement, you can see the dark orb and snake eye dots in his hand

Dots- back of flight helmet, and a thief's hockey mask; a likely enough flaunt spinning off the Vader dots, above at right, caught at an earlier robbery that linked to another crime same time frame.

Signals or just spooky cloth/dot coincidences? Given the timing and other surrounding crime/war circumstances surrounding them, they're enemy organized crime 'chat'. The Darth Vader, in USA, arrangement linked to a crime and name of Vader up here. Opposition is enemy to them, so my viewpoint is not politically correct nor near polite enough for them and those orbs with the dots for eyes? Are now in their experts' terms just orbs of going global and *Ecumenical*, …nice and slow see. Enemy camps have this 'evil eye' anti spy fixation.

Edmonton Police Chief Mike Boyd, 2010

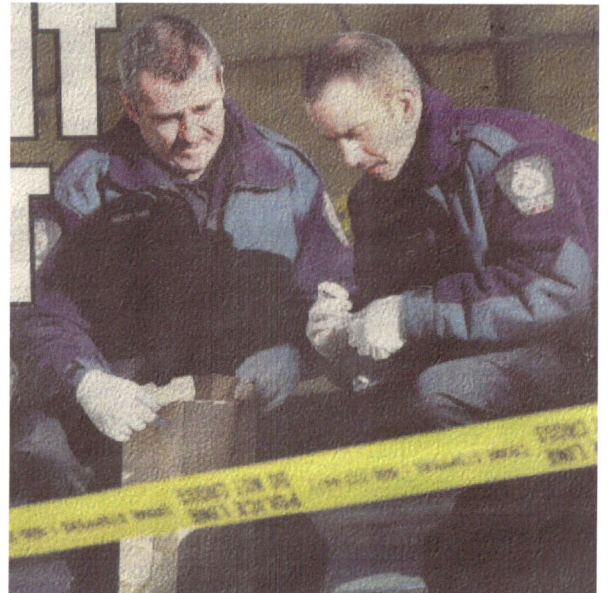

Edmonton, Alberta Cops- Halloween 2010

Houdini Theme *cuffs*, Vampire/Were wolf *silver bullet*; Sea Creature - *spray of bullets*

Edmonton Fire Dept with snake/hose Remote Viewing themes

Fire truck - yellow / dark red

New guided missile Destroyer, USS Jason Dunham, named for
Medal of Honour Recipient Cpl. Jason Dunham

Gave his life in 2004, as a Marine in Operation Iraqi Freedom, by throwing himself on top of a grenade to save the lives of two of his buddies; awarded the Medal of Honour Posthumously; Ghostly Visitation to the Viewer 1ˢᵗ 5ᵗʰ, in time synch quantum Psi fashion for the ship naming ceremony, Nov 5ᵗʰ, 2010

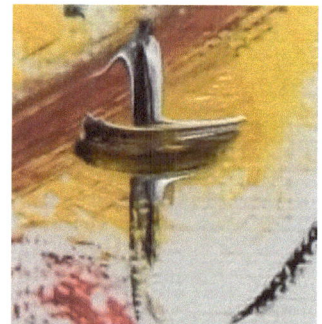

Marine Cpl Jason Dunham; RV bottom right at end of emote figure; silver bullet RV
As an identifier for the time synch of the recent Halloween, and the new visual reference, it's an RV descriptive, of the 'Jason' bogey man in the movie 'Halloween'. That's not linking this Jason except by an indication of surrounding events & his name.

Crow's Nest, with RV;   Ship commissioned in Honor of Hero Marine - USS Jason Dunham

CF-18 Hornet jet seeded sky trails/ Sun Fire Ops photos by 1st 5th, Edmonton, AB

CF-18 Hornet Jet , Psi Paintings by 1st 5th. Match to - *Cruise* (on You Tube)

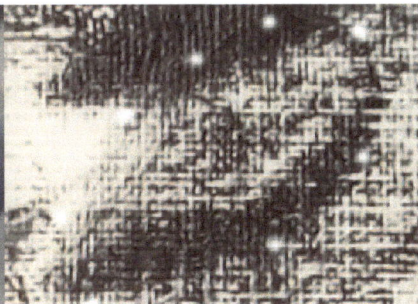

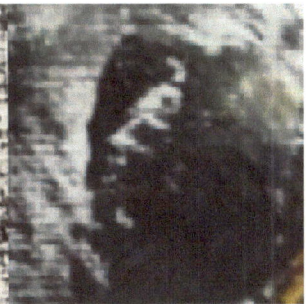

(USA) Spyland's NSA National Security (aka 'no such agency'), face RV, hand signal; during Yemen package bombs incident Oct. 2010

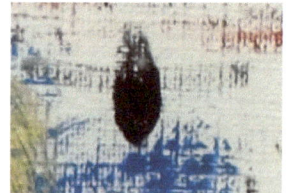

Edmonton Alberta, Cdn sky smoke signals; sky trails & swatch RV/emote

Edmonton Clock Tower, old Post Office Whyte Ave; evening sky

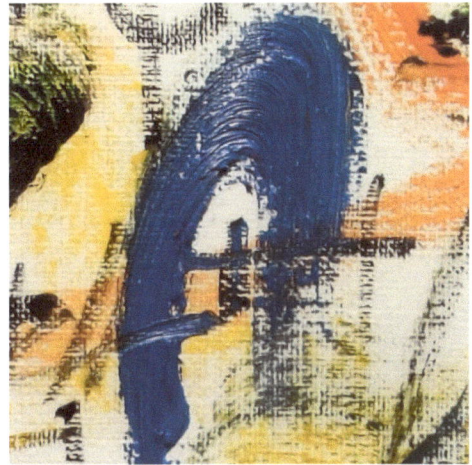

'Above the Law' starring Steven Seagal RV of head on car; gun with rounded stock; 'Dragnet' with Dan Akroyd - matching gun

Ted Nugent, concert in WV, USA; grey hat and gun at right, note the small but well formed gun RV

Canadian Wolf

Police - Long Beach, California - Car chase, ended as it spun out

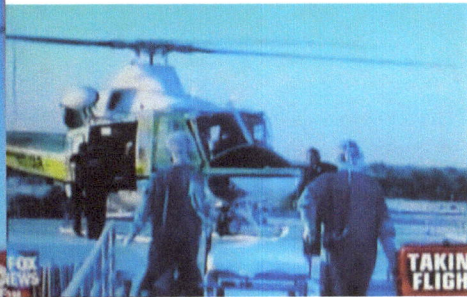

Coaxial Helicopter - greatly increased speed; new on the horizon

Donald Trump, star of the hit show 'The Apprentice'; RV 'punching fists' visuals

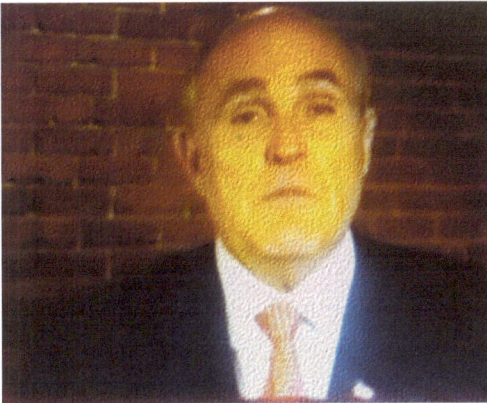
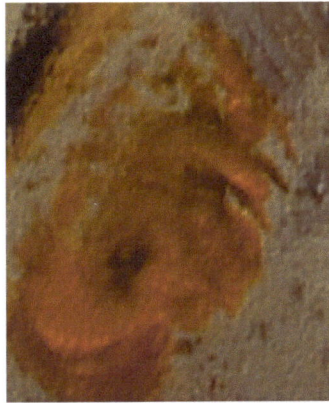
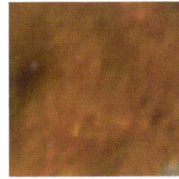

Fmr Mayor of New York Rudy Giuliani; hen party RV theme on 'View' popular tv show

Current Mayor of New York, Michael Bloomberg, with full portraiture RV in between white dots

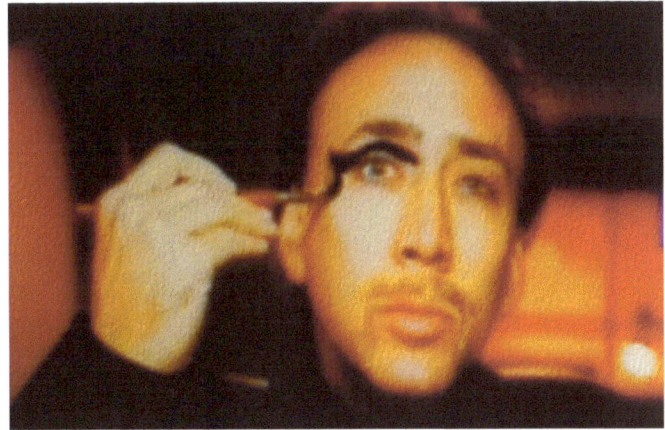

InterPol   International Police   Nicholas Cage

Russian T-50

The enemy forces are using the ignorance of the people not being told right by the officials and media to merge like in Somalia the bull horn, they are merging anti war with 'save the environment' it's a one two punch on our side's prosperity and system…Here they are attacking the German Police over Nuclear Fuel delivery

Car bombing, Mexico just over the US border; Col O North (Fox- War Stories') border fence ridge

Nov 8, 2010 Mexican Marines take out drug Cartel Kingpin 'Tony Tormento' (Tony Storm) huge deal - 3 hours of fighting; 150 Marines, 3 helicopters, 17 vehicles, to get it handled ...Upper Right -beheading RV

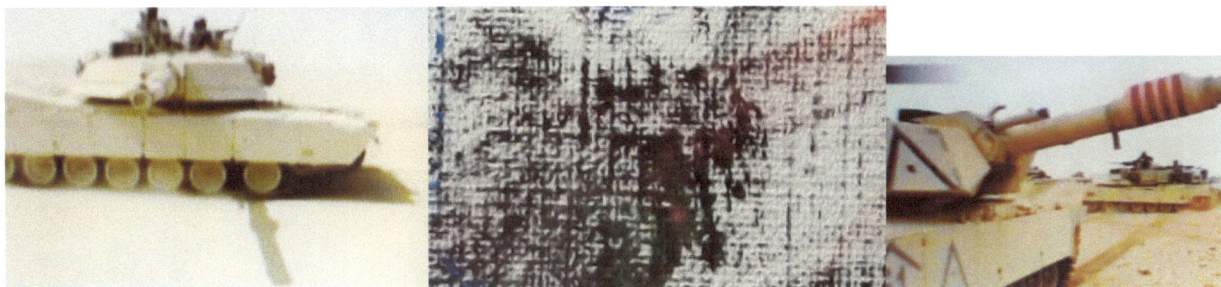

US - M/ A/ Tanks & RV

Edmonton downtown   Cowboy Round up   2010

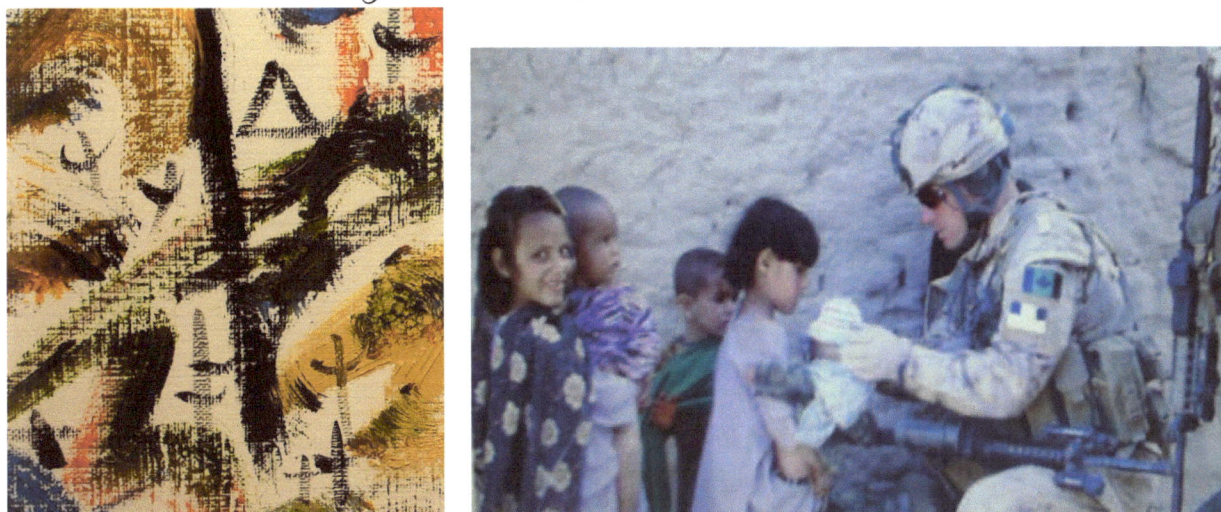

Canadian Soldier helping the Afghani future   2010

Gary Sinise - AVDLM. org American Veterans Disabled for Life Memorial . Org

Gen George Casey, Army Chief of Staff, hand signal, thumb tip, long fingers

CF-18 Hornet Jet Trail - X - over Q5 Leap

Edmonton, Alberta, Canada CF-18 Sky Trails

Sitting dog

Edmonton, Alberta, Canada CF-18 Sky Trails

Sitting dog

Canadian Troops in Afghanistan, November 11th, 2010

Barrel length looking downward into page; bullet Q5 Leap psi paint

Shanghai Knights starring Jackie Chan & Owen Wilson, with Psi links to Houdini,

UK hostages release; the English Royals, Prince William & Harry;

Psi paint views of ye Knights of olden tymes.

Houdini passing by, showed up as a slight shift in the lid that my Psi vision caught while we were doing the movie 'Shanghai Knights' up as per the old training years, when I would have to match the pre-done psi painting to the movie, when the movie locked up, and it wouldn't keep playing again until my vision made a visual match between it and the exact pixel configuration of the movie film's visuals. For example if I had painted the left top corner tip of a box then I would have to see that in the painting then look at the exact few pixels on the computer screen that formed the precise match, in order for the block to be released and the movie to continue on.

Sounds simple? It was an arduous process and we did it for all the relevant news clips and information that Spyland and the rest of them wanted me to release too. Their selection of daily visual release; live real time events included as well. Well established that Q5 leap runs a day or so ahead as a matter of precognitive routine. My psi painting often and full time, was resolving to the next days articles and events of significance. With the painting from the day before, these are done daily, being the one with the match for the computer pixel visual release. Precognition confirmed, beyond any doubt as to mere pattern chaos like pebbles on the side of the road, being the reason for such continuous matching. There was no question, it was extremely precision oriented.

A lot of the process involves Quantum chromo dynamics, and light info packets of an holistic nature, with the significance mainly focused on security, and motion. Freeze framing bits and pieces that match with tips and clues for the ones decoding the info that is contained in each days trained Psi painting as well as the running script we do as Remote Viewers. Gleaning for the odd the outstanding the precision glimpse ahead. Or as often, behind like the fingerprints relevance at the scene of a crime. Providing valuable hindsight matches.

In this instance it was during such a movie frame lock up freeze time, while I was looking for the correct combination of pixel information to match the visuals to the psi painting, that there was a forward again motion of the movie, but only for the briefest of moments. With some other locks and keys links having happened as well during this time frame, I understood the fleetness of the motion before the movie did a freeze frame again, ie: blocked, briefly unblocked, then quickly blocked again, hence I took the motion to indicate in RV terms, a descriptive for 'slight of hand' - a perceived strong Houdini marker. Given also in the movie, the additional letters over the trunk scene where they both were IN the opened trunk, with my at that time seeing it Psi, reading of *Hold n* as Houdini! A precision Remote View moment of understanding. Correctly as it turned out, as such precision Views are, they in real life in fact released the UK hostages the Pirates had held onto for one long year, let go that very day! Sure, that's definitely a link. A solid link.

 Not the first time I saw him do it, show up around a release like a ghostly marker enjoying it… tuning in…watching. Houdini died on Halloween, Oct 31, and he had apparently promised his widow to return to make contact. Séance being the thrill of those times. He was known as well to have helped with training the Military back then with the art of escapism, for real. They often are the Military ghosts that pass by here. Not spooky, just quietly making themselves availed of the Oracle to tune in on occasion. In true fascinating Q5 Leap manner, that was a definite Houdini moment, With Jackie Chan at the moving lid of the artefact dragon box and the precision marker of both Owen Wilson and Jackie Chan in the trunk with the letters over it. It was shut and slightly raised is how I think it went. For the shift when it happened. I remember I was sitting looking at the box closed. For a long time, couldn't make the visual match, then there was a very fast slight but real shift.

I read that up top as Houdini (it was not it was just close, hold on or no or something hold north who knows I saw hold and n…something but my psi said Houdini and look IN the trunk and when they move there are Fans there. A fan. Oh and London England right on it. I think the RV is starting to pull together PROOF and now it's actually showing more. That's so cool. It's QUANTUM info packets. They're complete. So if the times are inclusive of proof more then it will be included. Now, that's handy. Finally. AND it shows these things morph expand, grow …we learn it's built in or inherent in the process.
Like that star map teaches me things on deciphering and linking. They teamed. And it surfaced to prove. Like October's timely (it was just in a junk box in the garage I have a few of them) I wasn't looking for it, I was looking casually since it was out there with the room mate moving things around, looking for that turins page I got the Oct and the door info. The Leap and Connect …time synchs. Yes, fascinating, all we need is *Spock* from *Star Trek*.

Shanghai Knights - starring Jackie Chan & Owen Wilson

Jackie Chan & Owen Wilson are Honorary Knights of Mars

Owen Wilson; blonde marker Q5 Leap psi painting

Dragon on box lid;   Q5 Leap psi view paints

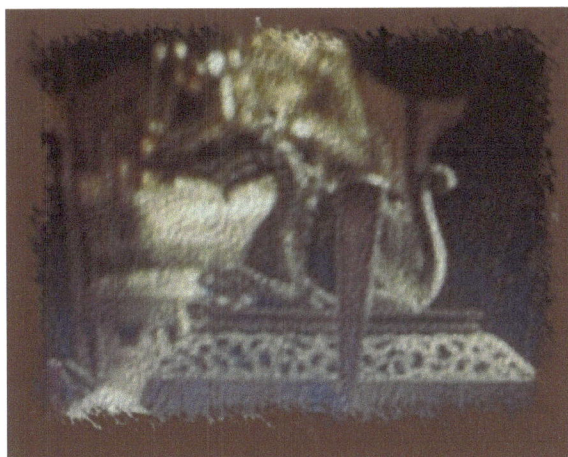

Blade edges

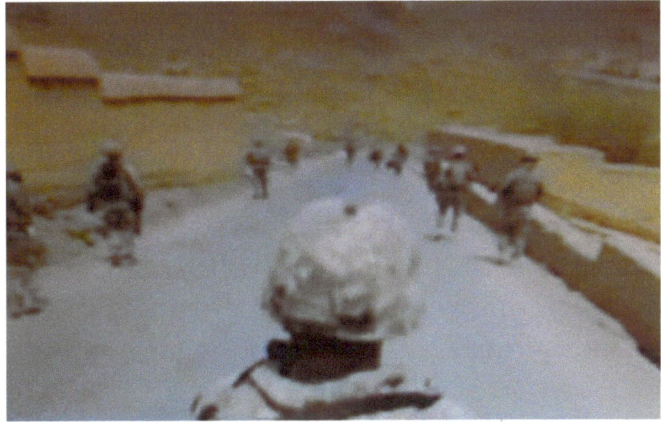

Time-synch to shadow play here in 'Shanghai Knights' clip; Afghan US troops, side steps

NY mosque note steps pattern top right; NY Times Square bomber, Mayday, steps at his place; Mayan pyramid the Serpent's Shadow; eg: use of Remote Viewing psychic paintings as they relate to Security

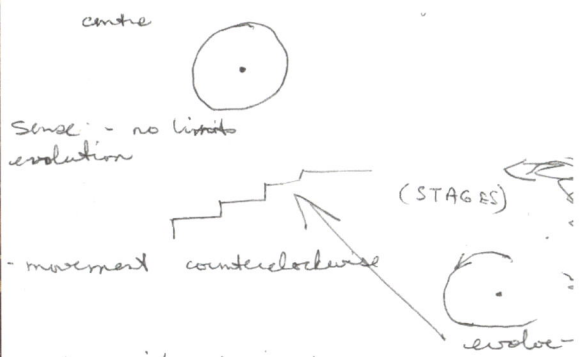

Chariot papyrus RV (excerpt) Double Orbs; RV by Psychic Octobrian Amethyst, Ont. Canada 1983

October's reading, another psychic, in Sept 1983, surfaced in typical Q5 Leap Time synch manner; note the two orbs the symbols for Sun. The Royals Prince Harry &

Prince William were linked into relevance during the time that this snippet of psychic reading came into play, Nov 14, 2010.

Relevant Remote Views of the Royals that also time synched in with the movie 'Shanghai Knights' starring Jackie Chan & Owen Wilson. The Knights visual imagery themes are all over their particular Viewing. *And*, I did my own rendition of Singing In The Rain that same day, prior to watching the movie Shanghai Knights where he was also singing the same song with that umbrella scene below. There is also this audio with the visuals, component to the Q5 Leap phenomenal quantum experience. That's why the script we do, running streaming commentary, with wild Psi to it as well comes in handy for tips too. If they know the surrounding circumstances, the authorities can find clues useful to them, often enough.

'Shanghai Knights' with Jackie Chan doing 'Singing In The Rain' with umbrella; matching RV

ʃmus s hat brim RV

Misty with British and Afghan troops; (below) camel whip and tip

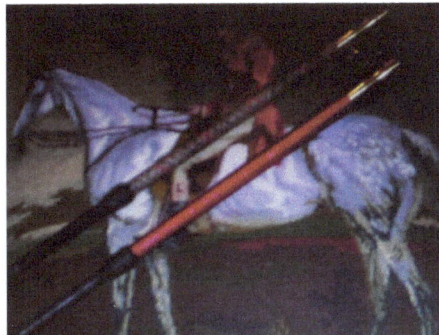

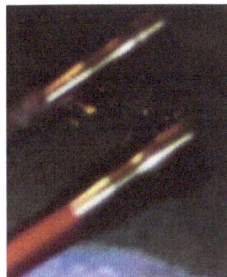

English Royalty -   Prince William & Prince Harry   - Sword/tips/Brim Q5 Leap

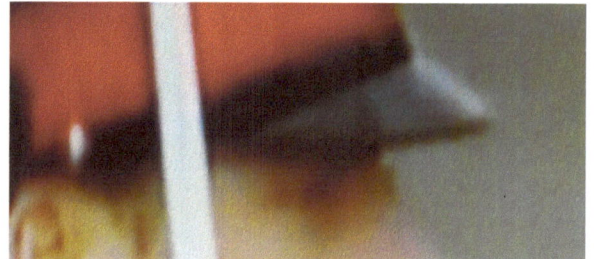

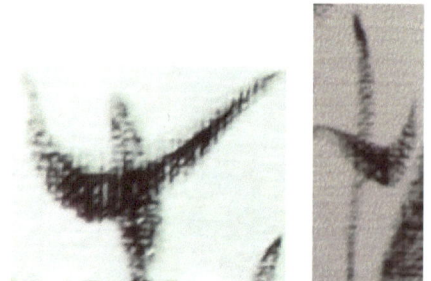

Point to brim on Royal caps, excerpt from Chariot papyrus RV

English Royal, Queen Elizabeth ǁ ;Queen Elizabeth ǁ diamond Tiara psi painting

English Prince Harry and Prince William

Prince - letter emote

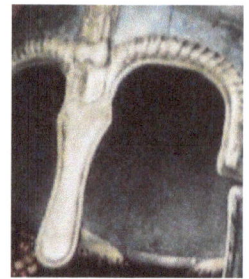

Sword tips;   Warrior s Helmet nose shield 3d RV psi paint

Pope Benedict XVI; new Cardinals Nov 20, 2010 similar helmet theme imagery following the Royals

Pope s emote

English engagement - Prince William & Kate Middleton

Engagement Prince William & Kate Middleton Nov 16ᵗʰ, 2010

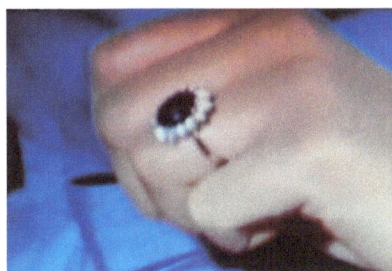

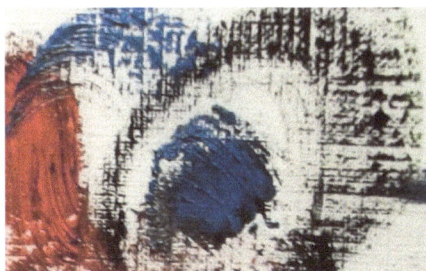

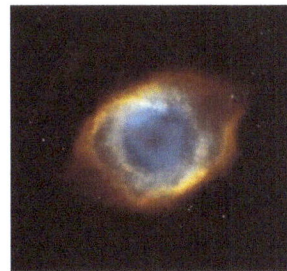

Princess Di s ring, Sapphire & Diamonds ; M57 Rng Nebula , RV link 2,000 Light Years from Earth

Larry s Lookout - Mars Rover s surface photos -RV diagonal match 2010; MARS vehicle troops Afghan

HOLE ON MARS

Canadian Military psi painting Afghanistan, 2010

(above left) at top right in 2006 psi paint and again in RV (above right)   Marching troops

Canadian Minister of Defence Peter MacKay; Psychic painting - side of hand

Cdn Minister of Defence Peter MacKay   Stealth & Jet purchases RV

Kiefer Sutherland star of hit show *24*; squared off hand signal while in Japan

Japanese Helmet & Bow; Sylvester Stallone s movie Rambo - Bow emote (above, right)

Samurai Sword - (central green diagonal)

24 starring Kiefer Sutherland - Movie poster -   Samurai Sword & gun RV - excerpt of gun

Canadian soldiers

Red Maple Leaf Flag tag RV

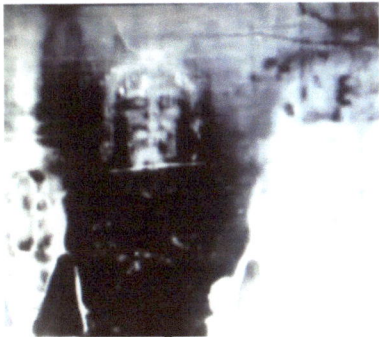

Turins Shroud RV match to 3d visual image of the face attributed to Jesus

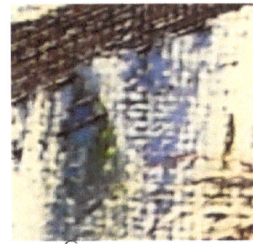

Treasury in movie Last Crusade starring Harrison Ford, ancient Petra associated RV; Holy Grail cup

‖ Chronicles Chapter V, verse 9

* And the priests brought in the ark of the covenant of the LORD unto his place, to the ORACLE of the house, into the most holy place, even under the wings of the Cherubims:

*For the Cherubims spread forth their wings over the place of the ark, and the Cherubims covered the ark and the staves thereof above.

*And they drew out the staves of the ark, that the ends of the staves were seen from the ark before the ORACLE: but they were not seen without.

         . . . And there it is unto this day.

Ark of the Covenant replica

Psi paint

Miami, Florida Cops   Q5 Leap   with guns drawn ; chased & stopped Robber; Brim emote

As formerly acknowledged all Police Officers are Honorary Knights of Mars

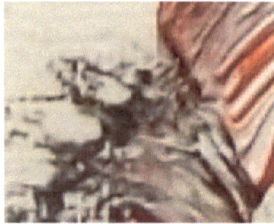

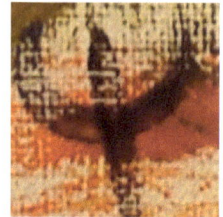

Edmonton, AB - Cops Chopper with visual emotes

US/Cdn Military

Royal Canadian Regiment

Brigadier General Dean Milner, Commander Joint Task Force Afghanistan, RV of gun butt

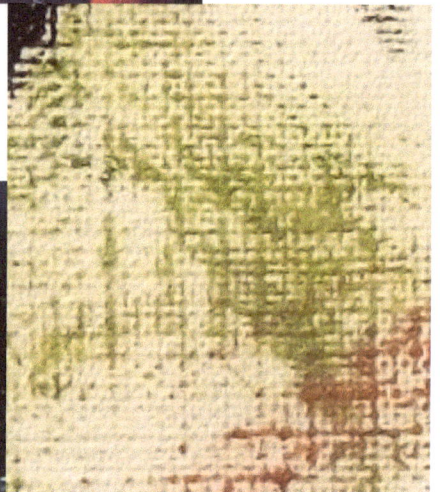

Sudden Impact - Dirty Harry - starring Clint Eastwood   **44 Magnum**

Barrel length looking downward into page; bullet Q5 Leap psi paint

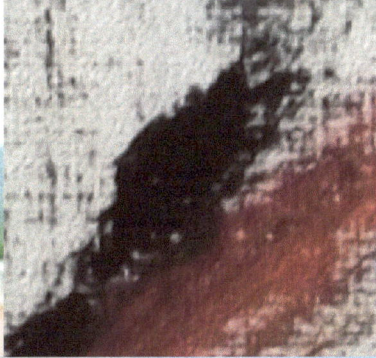

X M 25   Super Gun - light & super precision firing   Now in Afghanistan

Gen Walter Sharp

CF-18 Hornet jet trails Swordfish visual pattern; on flight deck USS George Washington

Star Wars starring Harrison Ford, C3P0 & R2D2; Space Explorer Sir Richard Branson visuals

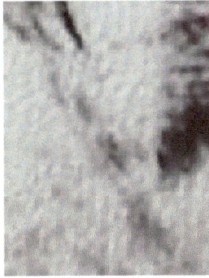

Canadian CF-18 Hornets flyby

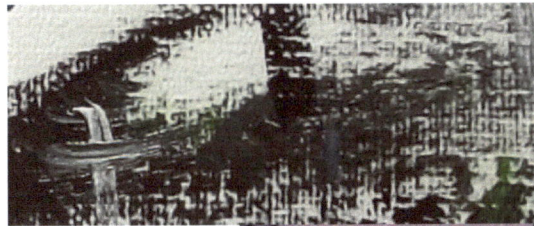

Row of jets Edmonton Grey Cup day nov 27th, 2010 flyby over tree tops, visual of row of dots Q5 Leap

Sunrise Edmonton AB Canada; jet flyer emotes

They started a few days ago, had me spill water into my new spiffy mint chocolate and emailed me a video clip of 'top ten low fly bys' starting with the Tom Cruise TOP GUN tower fly by ...and I was going yeah right as if Tom 's coming by here...then they did a jets fly by a row of them they held me back (we use secret ops tools) and I just got the dots over the trees. I was happy when they matched the RV for that day...then the next day they did a Side swipe with jets I just barely caught....more Grey Cup fun and games. That evening I went to the store and it happened -

Tom Cruise - KNIGHT & DAY - shining Limousine real life drive by PHANTOM OPS

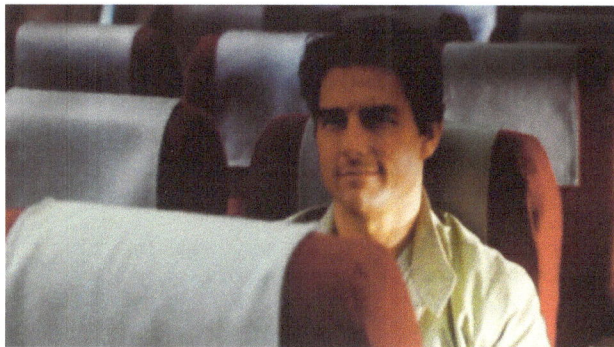

KNIGHT & DAY starring TOM CRUISE - cross weave seat/window/plane & wheel touchdown in real life

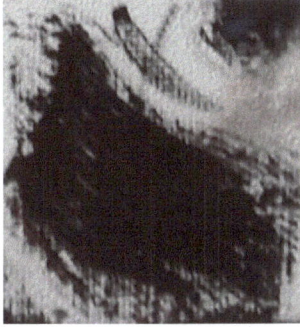

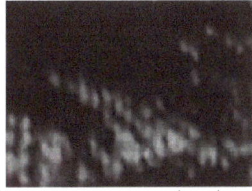

TC plane (wheel) touching down for the Edmonton Grey Cup 2010; TC face lower right corner black tinted limo windows -Psi Paint match to real Phantom Ops Cruise drive-by for 1st 5th

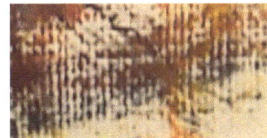

Pirates chat matching PARROT , Bulls running matching horns visuals, GUNS (upper row, far right)

Action car chase; land visual for SOMEDAY

Stripes on Bow tip – Black and Gold Eagle tip colors: Eagle from Iraq to USA

Road Warrior starring Mel Gibson

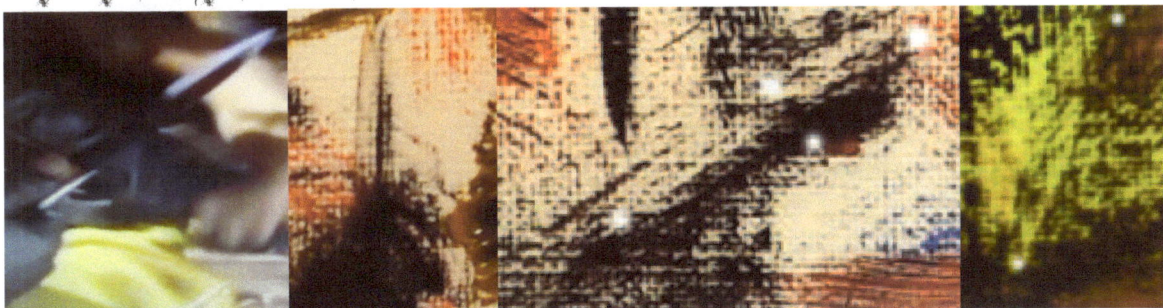

assortment of knives Psychic paintings by 1st 5th (arbitrary dots are to help you see the items outlined)

Flintlock Pistol RV; *Predator 2* movie starring Danny Glover

Ghost Ship & rowing RV; Ship with Canon RV

Samural Sword sideways visual; Operation Keen Sword - US and Japan Military drill

THE EXPENDABLES starring Sylvester Stallone & Jason Statham

(Bottom, left of center) Knife being thrown by Jason Statham - center Bullseye ending

Visual Psychic painting of Sylvester Stallone with two guns parallel

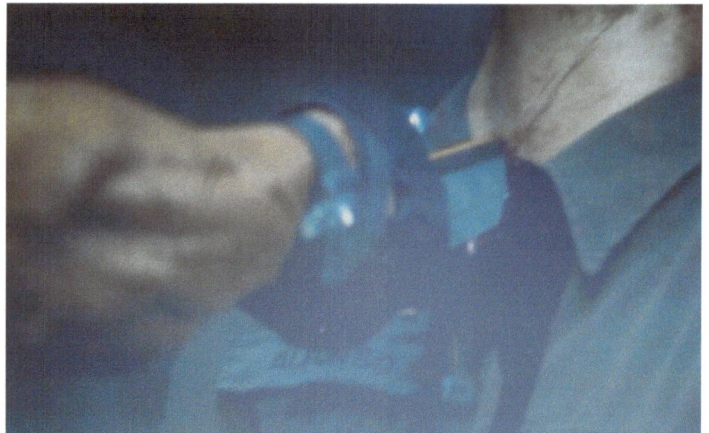

Sylvester Stallone knife in throat/ grr with window glass

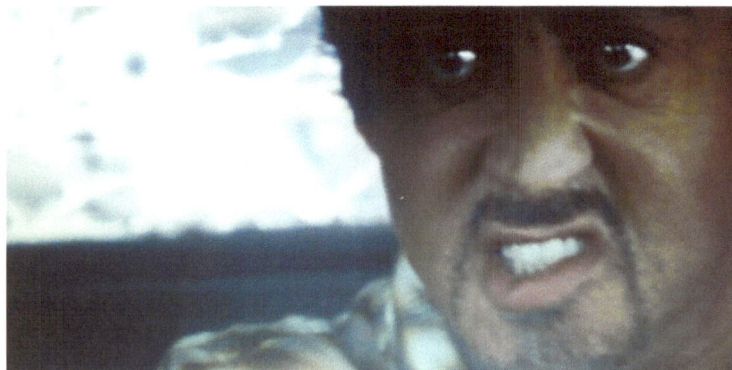

Jet Li

Man falling/arches; Sword RV

Expendables extreme action scene & RV; Knife toss by Jason Statham

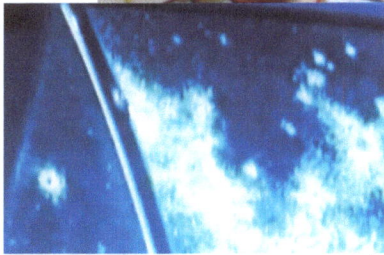

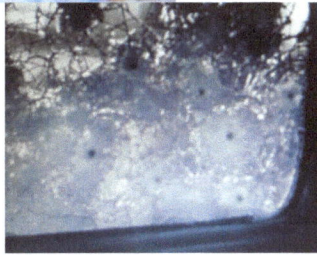

SW US & Mexico border trouble boiling over National Guard, Sheriff Babeu, Pinal County Arizona

RV bullet hole visuals - SW and real is on the left, the movie Expendables is on the right

Hidalgo starring Viggo Mortensen - Remote View of Lariat; Canadian soldier with large gun

'Mad' magazine classic SPY VS SPY ; Real Deal #1 (above, right)

Real Deal #1 - RV of bike fender - Nov 29th 2010, two spies on bikes attached bombs to the car windows of Iranian nuclear scientists...Iran has been secretly shipping arms and proliferating, raising the threat of nuclear hostility ....

Real Deal #2 - Psychic doing a pixel release on the New Zealand de Havilland DHC-4 Caribou aircraft

http://www.youtube.com/watch?v=kjrRhg-_Lxw

Rattle

" ...I will always remember God's promise, that while step after step may be hard and halting, the whole of the journey will be my most divine reward."

Sylvia Browne "Blessings From the Other Side"

Ship & 3d paint blue sharks tooth

glimpse of Psychic discipline Future Phantom Ops for wounded warriors; exoskeleton - RE WALK

Wounded warrior emote - Phantom Ops/Psi Warriors

Ancient

Lean, sleek, deadly...
Softly purring of power rhythms.
Resounding to ancient tunes
Played instinctually,
Round fires of purity.

As truths unfold,
A pole star glistening,
To purposes, indifferent
Bundles of raw objectivity.

Obsessed with the night,
Exchanging furtive glances.
Disappearing into dimensions
Replenishing an arduous nature.

Golden on blackness
As footprints pad shadows
And hunger is filled.

Slinking through and beyond
New territorial boundaries.
To conquer with majesty
Often elusive, time's mystery.

Gardena CA cops

Match the dots to see this bag head tilting the gun to show us the Precision ancient Remote View in this Chariot papyrus excerpt; confirmation they access intel material, but not news

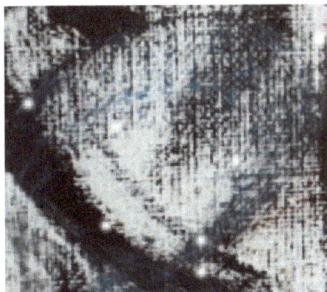

Kingdom of the Crystal Skull starring Harrison Ford & Karen Allen

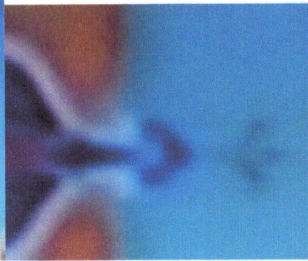

Iran's Ahmadinejad with chat visuals; possibly linked to the Blue Mosque in Toronto which has a notably radical non-integration mandate exhibited by their long comprehensive list that their followers in Canada are not allowed to participate in celebrations; note plane visual approaching the coast from the right, linked to the older remote view 2007 training paint by 1st 5th (excerpt, above right) which apparently they have access to, a fact known for some time.

The real, not the hijacked meaning, of that Psi paint by myself, was S for South, a compass direction. And that's a Cross not a 'plane' they are reading them falsely. Beware false prophets.

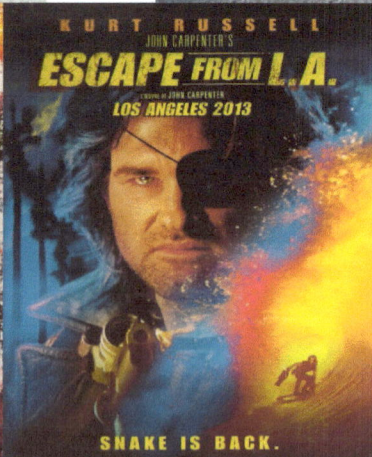

Escape From LA & Escape From NY starring Kurt Russell of the original Stargate

www.ingramcontent.com/pod-product-compliance
Lightning Source LLC
Chambersburg PA
CBHW061054090426
42742CB00002B/38